To Bee...
With Love —
12/2000

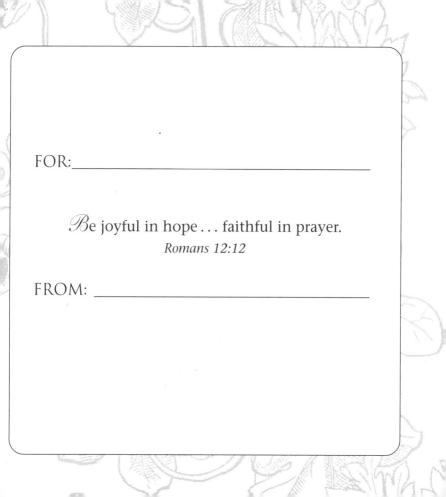

FOR:_____

*B*e joyful in hope . . . faithful in prayer.
Romans 12:12

FROM: _____

Prayers for a Woman of Faith
Copyright © 1998 by New Life Clinics
ISBN 0-310-97336-8

Requests for information should be addressed to: ZondervanPublishingHouse
Mail Drop B20
Grand Rapids, Michigan 49530
http://www.zondervan.com

Senior Editor: Joy Marple
Project Editor: Jessica & Sarah Hupp
Art Director: Jody Langley

Printed in China
99 00 01 /HK/ 11 10

Prayers
for a
Woman
of Faith

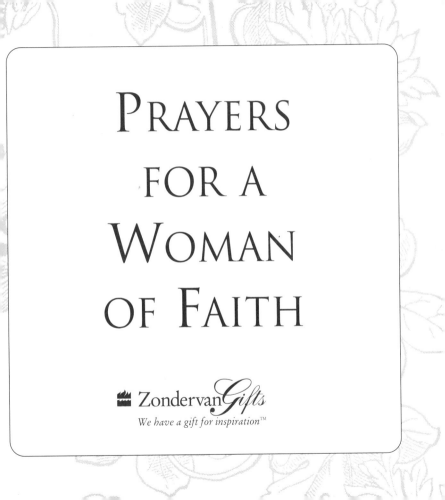

Zondervan*Gifts*

We have a gift for inspiration™

PRAYERS FOR A WOMAN OF FAITH ON

The Lord's Prayer

*O*ur Father in heaven, hallowed be your name, your kingdom come, your will be done on earth as it is in heaven. Give us today our daily bread. Forgive us our debts, as we also have forgiven our debtors. And lead us not into temptation, but deliver us from evil; for yours is the kingdom and the power and the glory forever. Amen.

Matthew 6:9–13

PRAYERS OF ASSURANCE

*W*hen I am afraid, I will trust in you, O God.

Psalm 56:3

O my Strength, I watch for you; you, O God, are my fortress, my loving God. God will go before me.

Psalm 59:9–10

❧

*T*urn your ear to me, O LORD, come quickly to my rescue; be my rock of refuge, a strong fortress to save me.

Psalm 31:2

*H*ave mercy on me, O God, have mercy on me, for in you my soul takes refuge. I will take refuge in the shadow of your wings until the disaster has passed.

Psalm 57:1

❧

*D*o not let the floodwaters engulf me or the depths swallow me up or the pit close its mouth over me. Answer me, O LORD, out of the goodness of your love; in your great mercy turn to me.

Psalm 69:15–16

$\mathcal{I}$ will remember the deeds of the LORD; yes, I will remember your miracles of long ago. I will meditate on all your works and consider all your mighty deeds. Your ways, O God, are holy. What god is so great as our God? You are the God who performs miracles; you display your power among the peoples.

Psalm 77:11–14

I will praise you, O Lord, with all my heart;
I will tell of all your wonders. I will be glad and
rejoice in you; I will sing praise to your name,
O Most High. My enemies turn back; they stumble
and perish before you. For you have upheld
my right and my cause; you have sat on your
throne, judging righteously.

Psalm 9:1–4

❧

*Y*ou are my lamp, O Lord; the Lord turns my
darkness into light. With your help I can advance
against a troop; with my God I can scale a wall.

2 Samuel 22:29–30

*N*ow, this is what the LORD says, "Fear not, for I have redeemed you; I have summoned you by name; you are mine. When you pass through the waters, I will be with you; and when you pass through the rivers, they will not sweep over you. When you walk through the fire, you will not be burned; the flames will not set you ablaze. For I am the LORD, your God, the Holy One of Israel, your Savior."

Isaiah 43:1–3

PRAYERS OF BLESSING

*T*he LORD bless you and keep you; the LORD
make his face shine upon you and be gracious
to you; the LORD turn his face toward you
and give you peace.

Numbers 6:24–26

*S*ave your people and bless your inheritance,
O LORD; be their shepherd and carry them forever.

Psalm 28:9

❧

*L*et all who take refuge in you be glad; let them
ever sing for joy. Spread your protection over them,
that those who love your name may rejoice in you.
For surely, O LORD, you bless the righteous; you
surround them with your favor as with a shield.

Psalm 5:11–12

*Y*ou answer us with awesome deeds of
righteousness, O God our Savior.

Psalm 65:5

❧

*P*raise the LORD, all his works everywhere in his
dominion. Praise the LORD, O my soul.

Psalm 103:22

*M*any, O Lord my God, are the wonders you have done. The things you planned for us no one can recount to you; were I to speak and tell of them, they would be too many to declare.

Psalm 40:5

❧

*B*lessed be your glorious name, O Lord, and may it be exalted above all blessing and praise.

Nehemiah 9:5

$\mathscr{I}$ have not turned aside from your commands nor have I forgotten any of them. I have obeyed the LORD my God; I have done everything you commanded me. Look down from heaven, your holy dwelling place, and bless your people.

Deuteronomy 26:13–15

❧

$\mathcal{L}$ORD, you have been our dwelling place throughout all generations. Before the mountains were born or you brought forth the earth and the world, from everlasting to everlasting you are God. Teach us to number our days aright, that we may gain a heart of wisdom. Satisfy us in the morning with your unfailing love, that we may sing for joy and be glad all our days. May your deeds be shown to your servants, your splendor to their children. May the favor of the LORD our God rest upon us; establish the work of our hands for us—yes, establish the work of our hands.

Psalm 90:1–2, 12, 14, 16–17

PRAYERS FOR BOLDNESS AND COURAGE

The LORD is my rock, my fortress and my deliverer; my God is my rock, in whom I take refuge. He is my shield and the horn of my salvation, my stronghold. I call to the LORD, who is worthy of praise, and I am saved from my enemies.

Psalm 18:2–3

I have set the LORD always before me. Because he is at my right hand, I will not be shaken.

Psalm 16:8

❧

*E*ven though I walk through the valley of the shadow of death, I will fear no evil, for you O LORD, are with me; your rod and your staff, they comfort me.

Psalm 23:4

❧

*T*he LORD is my light and my salvation—whom shall I fear? The LORD is the stronghold of my life—of whom shall I be afraid?

Psalm 27:1

*F*or in the day of trouble [the LORD] will keep me safe in his dwelling; he will hide me in the shelter of his tabernacle and set me high upon a rock.

Psalm 27:5

❧

O LORD, you will hear the desire of the meek; you will strengthen their heart, you will incline your ear to do justice for the orphan and the oppressed, so that those from the earth may strike terror no more.

Psalm 10:17–18 (NRSV)

*M*y enemies turn back; they stumble and perish before you O LORD. For you have upheld my right and my cause; you have sat on your throne, judging righteously. You have rebuked the nations and destroyed the wicked; you have blotted out their name for ever and ever.

Psalm 9:3–5

$\mathcal{D}$o not be afraid or discouraged. The
battle is not yours, but God's. Stand firm
and see the deliverance the LORD will give you.
Do not be afraid; do not be discouraged.
The LORD will be with you.

2 Chronicles 20:15, 17

$\mathcal{T}$hey raised their voices together in prayer to God. "Sovereign Lord, you made the heaven and the earth and the sea, and everything in them. You spoke by the Holy Spirit through the mouth of your servant, our father David: "'Why do the nations rage and the peoples plot in vain? The kings of the earth take their stand and the rulers gather together against the Lord and against his Anointed One.' They did what your power and will had decided beforehand should happen. Now, Lord, consider their threats and enable your servants to speak your word with great boldness. Stretch out your hand to heal and perform miraculous signs and wonders through the name of your holy servant Jesus."

Acts 4:24–26, 28–30

PRAYERS OF COMFORT

My comfort in my suffering is this: Your
promise preserves my life, O Lord.
Psalm 119:50

My soul faints with longing for your salvation,
but I have put my hope in your word, O Lord.
Psalm 119:81

I will praise you, O LORD, among the nations;
I will sing praises to your name.
2 Samuel 22:50

❧

*F*or surely, O LORD, you bless the righteous; you
surround them with your favor as with a shield.
Psalm 5:12

❧

*Y*ou guide me with your counsel, O LORD,
and afterward you will take me into glory.
Psalm 73:24

$\mathscr{Y}$ou will keep in perfect peace him whose mind
is steadfast, because he trusts in you, O God.
Isaiah 26:3

❧

$\mathscr{Y}$ou come to the help of those who gladly do
right, who remember your ways, O God.
Isaiah 64:5

❧

"$\mathscr{A}$s a mother comforts her child, so will I
comfort you; and you will be comforted,"
says the LORD.
Isaiah 66:13

*T*he LORD is my rock, my fortress and my deliverer; my God is my rock, in whom I take refuge, my shield and the horn of my salvation. He is my stronghold, my refuge and my savior— from violent men you save me. I call to the LORD, who is worthy of praise, and I am saved from my enemies. The waves of death swirled about me; the torrents of destruction overwhelmed me. The cords of the grave coiled around me; the snares of death confronted me. In my distress I called to the LORD; I called out to my God. From his temple he heard my voice; my cry came to his ears.

2 Samuel 22:2–7

*F*or you, O LORD, have delivered my soul from death, my eyes from tears, my feet from stumbling, that I may walk before the LORD in the land of the living.

Psalm 116:8–9

*E*ven though I walk through the valley of the shadow of death, I will fear no evil, for you O LORD are with me; your rod and your staff, they comfort me.

Psalm 23:4

I will be glad and rejoice in your love O LORD, for you saw my affliction and knew the anguish of my soul. You have not handed me over to the enemy but have set my feet in a spacious place.

Psalm 31:7–8

❧

F ind rest, O my soul, in God alone; my hope comes from him. He alone is my rock and my salvation; he is my fortress, I will not be shaken.

Psalm 62:5–6

PRAYERS OF CONFESSION

*S*overeign LORD, forgive!

Amos 7:2

O my God, I am too ashamed and disgraced
to lift up my face to you, my God, because our
sins are higher than our heads and our guilt
has reached to the heavens.

Ezra 9:6

I acknowledged my sin to you and did not cover up my iniquity. I said, "I will confess my transgressions to the LORD"—and you forgave the guilt of my sin.

Psalm 32:5

❧

*G*od, have mercy on me, a sinner.

Luke 18:13

❧

I have sinned greatly in what I have done. Now, O LORD, I beg you, take away the guilt of your servant. I have done a very foolish thing.

2 Samuel 24:10

*W*ho is a God like you, who pardons sin and forgives the transgression of the remnant of his inheritance? You do not stay angry forever but delight to show mercy. You will again have compassion on us; you will tread our sins underfoot and hurl all our iniquities into the depths of the sea.

Micah 7:18–19

❧

O LORD, teach me what I cannot see; if I have done wrong, I will not do so again.

Job 34:32

❧

*H*ave mercy on me, O God, according to your unfailing love; according to your great compassion blot out my transgressions. Wash away all my iniquity and cleanse me from my sin. For I know my transgressions, and my sin is always before me. Against you, you only, have I sinned and done what is evil in your sight, so that you are proved right when you speak and justified when you judge. Surely I was sinful at birth, sinful from the time my mother conceived me. Surely you desire truth in the inner parts; you teach me wisdom in the inmost place. Cleanse me with hyssop, and I will be clean; wash me, and I will be whiter than snow. Let me hear joy and gladness; let the bones you have crushed rejoice. Hide your face from my sins and blot out all my iniquity. Create in me a pure heart, O God, and renew a steadfast spirit within me. Do not cast me from your presence or take your Holy Spirit from me. Restore to me the joy of your salvation and grant me a willing spirit, to sustain me.

Psalm 51:1–12

O LORD, the great and awesome God, who keeps his covenant of love with all who love him and obey his commands, we have sinned and done wrong. We have been wicked and have rebelled; we have turned away from your commands and laws. The LORD our God is merciful and forgiving, even though we have rebelled against him. Now, our God, hear the prayers and petitions of your servant. We do not make requests of you because we are righteous, but because of your great mercy.

Daniel 9:4–5, 9, 17–18

PRAYERS OF DEDICATION

O LORD, how I long for your precepts! Preserve my
life in your righteousness.

Psalm 119:40

*P*reserve my life according to your love, O LORD,
and I will obey the statutes of your mouth.

Psalm 119:88

*H*ear my voice in accordance with your love;
preserve my life, O LORD, according to your laws.

Psalm 119:149

❧

*Y*our compassion is great, O LORD; preserve my
life according to your laws.

Psalm 119:156

*I*nto your hands I commit my spirit; redeem me,
O LORD, the God of truth.

Psalm 31:5

≈

*S*how me your ways, O LORD, teach me your
paths; guide me in your truth and teach me,
for you are God my Savior, and my hope is in
you all day long.

Psalm 25:4–5

*B*ring joy to your servant, for to you,
O LORD, I lift up my soul.

Psalm 86:4

❧

*T*each me your way, O LORD, and I will walk
in your truth; give me an undivided heart, that I
may fear your name.

Psalm 86:11

*L*et the morning bring me word of your unfailing love, for I have put my trust in you. Show me the way I should go, for to you I lift up my soul. Teach me to do your will, for you are my God; may your good Spirit lead me on level ground.

Psalm 143:8, 10

❧

*T*o you, O LORD, I lift up my soul.

Psalm 25:1

*W*hom have I in heaven but you? And earth has nothing I desire besides you. My flesh and my heart may fail, but God is the strength of my heart and my portion forever.

Psalm 73:25–26

*S*earch me, O God, and know my heart; test me and know my anxious thoughts. See if there is any offensive way in me, and lead me in the way everlasting.

Psalm 139:23–24

PRAYERS OF FORGIVENESS

O LORD, forgive my hidden faults. Keep your
servant also from willful sins; may they not
rule over me. Then will I be blameless,
innocent of great transgression.

Psalm 19:12–13

*O*ur Father, forgive us our debts, as we also
have forgiven our debtors.

Matthew 6:12

❧

*R*emember not the sins of my youth and
my rebellious ways; according to your love
remember me, for you are good, O LORD.
Good and upright is the LORD; therefore
he instructs sinners in his ways.

Psalm 25:7–8

*F*or the sake of your name, O LORD, forgive my
iniquity, though it is great.

Psalm 25:11

❧

O LORD, look upon my affliction and my distress
and take away all my sins.

Psalm 25:18

❧

I acknowledged my sin to you and did not
cover up my iniquity. I said, "I will confess my
transgressions to the LORD,"—and you forgave
the guilt of my sin.

Psalm 32:5

*H*ide your face from my sins and blot out all my iniquity. Create in me a pure heart, O God, and renew a steadfast spirit within me. Do not cast me from your presence or take your Holy Spirit from me. Restore to me the joy of your salvation and grant me a willing spirit, to sustain me.

Psalm 51:9–12

❧

*W*hen we were overwhelmed by sins, you forgave our transgressions. O LORD, blessed are those you choose and bring near to live in your courts! We are filled with the good things of your house, of your holy temple.

Psalm 65:3–4

*H*elp us, O God our Savior, for the glory of
your name; deliver us and forgive our sins
for your name's sake.

Psalm 79:9

❧

*Y*ou forgave the iniquity of your people and
covered all their sins. You set aside all your wrath
and turned from your fierce anger. Restore us
again, O God our Savior, and put away your
displeasure toward us.

Psalm 85:2–4

$\mathcal{Y}$ou are forgiving and good, O LORD, abounding
in love to all who call to you.

Psalm 86:5

✼

$\mathcal{F}$or the sake of your name, O LORD, forgive my
iniquity, though it is great.

Psalm 25:11

PRAYERS FOR GUIDANCE

*T*each me your way, O LORD, and I will walk
in your truth; give me an undivided heart,
that I may fear your name.

Psalm 86:11

*I*f you are pleased with me, O LORD, teach me your ways so I may know you and continue to find favor with you.

Exodus 33:13

❧

*S*how me your ways, O LORD, teach me your paths; guide me in your truth and teach me, for you are God my Savior, and my hope is in you all day long.

Psalm 25:4–5

❧

O LORD open my eyes that I may see wonderful things in your law.

Psalm 119:18

O Lord, send forth your light and your truth,
let them guide me; let them bring me to your
holy mountain, to the place where you dwell.

Psalm 43:3

*T*each me, O Lord, to follow your decrees;
then I will keep them to the end. Give me
understanding, and I will keep your law and obey
it with all my heart. Direct me in the path of your
commands, for there I find delight. Turn my heart
toward your statutes and not toward selfish gain.
Turn my eyes away from worthless things;
preserve my life according to your word.

Psalm 119:33–37

O Lord, direct my footsteps according to your
word; let no sin rule over me.

Psalm 119:133

❧

S earch me, O God, and know my heart;
test me and know my anxious thoughts.
See if there is any offensive way in me,
and lead me in the way everlasting.

Psalm 139:23–24

*T*each me what I cannot see, O LORD; if I have
done wrong, I will not do so again.

Job 34:32

❧

*T*each me knowledge and good judgment
O God, for I believe in your commands.

Psalm 119:66

❧

O LORD, teach me, and I will be quiet; show me
where I have been wrong.

Job 6:24

$\mathcal{L}$et the morning bring me word of your unfailing love, for I have put my trust in you. Show me the way I should go, for to you I lift up my soul. Rescue me from my enemies, O LORD, for I hide myself in you. Teach me to do your will, for you are my God; may your good Spirit lead me on level ground.

Psalm 143:8–10

❧

$\mathcal{L}$ead me, O LORD, in your righteousness because of my enemies—make straight your way before me.

Psalm 5:8

*T*each me your way, O LORD, and I will
walk in your truth; give me an undivided
heart, that I may fear your name.

Psalm 86:11

❧

I recounted my ways and you answered me;
teach me your decrees. O LORD, let me understand
the teaching of your precepts; then I will
meditate on your wonders.

Psalm 119:26–27

*F*rom the ends of the earth I call to you,
O LORD, I call as my heart grows faint; lead me
to the rock that is higher than I.

Psalm 61:2

❧

*S*ince you are my rock and my fortress, for the
sake of your name lead and guide me. Free me
from the trap that is set for me, for you are my
refuge. Into your hands I commit my spirit;
redeem me, O LORD, the God of truth.

Psalm 31:3–5

*W*here can I go from your Spirit? Where can I flee from your presence? If I go up to the heavens, you are there; if I make my bed in the depths, you are there. If I rise on the wings of the dawn, if I settle on the far side of the sea, even there your hand will guide me, your right hand will hold me fast.

Psalm 139:7–10

O God, you guide me with your counsel, and
afterward you will take me into glory.

Psalm 73:24

❧

Teach us to number our days aright, O God,
that we may gain a heart of wisdom.

Psalm 90:12

❧

Lord, teach us to pray.

Luke 11:1

PRAYERS OF HEALING, RESTORATION, AND PEACE

O LORD my God, I called to you for help
and you healed me.

Psalm 30:2

$\mathscr{B}$e merciful to me, LORD, for I am faint; O LORD,
heal me, for my bones are in agony.

Psalm 6:2

✸

$\mathscr{R}$estore me, and I will return, because you are
the LORD my God.

Jeremiah 31:18

$\mathscr{P}$raise the LORD, O my soul, and forget not all his benefits—who forgives all your sins and heals all your diseases.

Psalm 103:2–3

❧

$\mathscr{O}$ LORD, have mercy on me; heal me, for I have sinned against you.

Psalm 41:4

❧

$\mathscr{H}$eal me, O LORD, and I will be healed; save me and I will be saved, for you are the one I praise.

Jeremiah 17:14

$\mathcal{L}$ord, you restored me to health and let me live. Surely it was for my benefit that I suffered such anguish. In your love you kept me from the pit of destruction; you have put all my sins behind your back. For the grave cannot praise you, death cannot sing your praise; those who go down to the pit cannot hope for your faithfulness. The living, the living—they praise you, as I am doing today; fathers tell their children about your faithfulness. The LORD will save me, and we will sing with stringed instruments all the days of our lives in the temple of the LORD.

Isaiah 38:16–20

PRAYERS OF INTERCESSION FOR OTHERS

*D*o good, O LORD, to those who are good, to those who are upright in heart.

Psalm 125:4

O LORD Almighty, God of Israel, enthroned between the cherubim, you alone are God over all the kingdoms of the earth. You have made heaven and earth. Give ear, O LORD, and hear; open your eyes, O LORD, and see.

Isaiah 37:16–17

❧

*N*ow, O LORD our God, deliver us from his hand, so that all kingdoms on earth may know that you alone, O LORD, are God.

Isaiah 37:20

❧

*T*hose of steadfast mind you keep in peace, O LORD, in peace because they trust in you.

Isaiah 26:3 (NRSV)

*M*ay God be gracious to us and bless us and make his face shine upon us, that your ways may be known on earth, your salvation among all nations.

Psalm 67:1–2

❧

*R*eturn to us, O God Almighty! Look down from heaven and see! Then we will not turn away from you; revive us, and we will call on your name. Restore us, O LORD God Almighty; make your face shine upon us, that we may be saved.

Psalm 80:14, 18–19

*T*urn to me and have mercy on me, O Lord, as you always do to those who love your name. Direct my footsteps according to your word; let no sin rule over me. Redeem me from the oppression of men, that I may obey your precepts. Make your face shine upon your servant and teach me your decrees.

Psalm 119:132–135

❧

*L*ord, you have been our dwelling place throughout all generations. Before the mountains were born or you brought forth the earth and the world, from everlasting to everlasting you are God.

Psalm 90:1–2

O LORD, restore to me the joy of your salvation and grant me a willing spirit, to sustain me.

Psalm 51:12

❧

*H*ave compassion on your servants, O LORD. Satisfy us in the morning with your unfailing love, that we may sing for joy and be glad all our days. Make us glad for as many days as you have afflicted us, for as many years as we have seen trouble. May your deeds be shown to your servants, your splendor to their children. May the favor of the LORD our God rest upon us; establish the work of our hands for us— yes, establish the work of our hands.

Psalm 90:13–17

Give attention to your servant's prayer and his plea for mercy, O LORD my God. Hear the cry and the prayer that your servant is praying in your presence this day. Hear the supplication of your servant and of your people—hear from heaven, your dwelling place, and when you hear, forgive. When the heavens are shut up and there is no rain because your people have sinned against you, and when they pray toward this place and confess your name and turn from their sin because you have afflicted them, then hear from heaven and forgive the sin of your servants. Teach them the right way to live, and send rain on the land you gave your people. Forgive and act; deal with each man according to all he does, since you know his heart (for you alone know the hearts of all men).

1 Kings 8:28, 30, 35–36, 39

❧

$\mathcal{B}$ring joy to your servant, for to you,
O LORD, I lift up my soul.

Psalm 86:4

❧

$\mathcal{L}$et the light of your face shine upon us, O LORD.
You have filled my heart with greater joy than when
their grain and new wine abound.

Psalm 4:6–7

❧

$\mathcal{L}$et all who take refuge in you be glad; let them
ever sing for joy. Spread your protection over them,
that those who love your name may rejoice in you.
For surely, O LORD, you bless the righteous; you
surround them with your favor as with a shield.

Psalm 5:11–12

*M*y heart is glad and my tongue rejoices; my body also will rest secure, because you, O LORD will not abandon me to the grave, nor will you let your Holy One see decay. You have made known to me the path of life; you will fill me with joy in your presence, with eternal pleasures at your right hand.

Psalm 16:9–11

❧

*Y*ou turned my wailing into dancing; you removed my sackcloth and clothed me with joy, that my heart may sing to you and not be silent. O LORD my God, I will give you thanks forever.

Psalm 30:11–12

*S*atisfy us in the morning with your unfailing
love, O LORD, that we may sing for joy and
be glad all our days.

Psalm 90:14

❧

*F*or you make me glad by your deeds, O LORD;
I sing for joy at the works of your hands. How
great are your works, O LORD, how profound
your thoughts!

Psalm 92:4–5

❧

I will lie down and sleep in peace, for you alone,
O LORD, make me dwell in safety.

Psalm 4:8

*G*reat peace have they who love your law, O God,
and nothing can make them stumble.

Psalm 119:165

❧

*H*ow great is your goodness, O LORD, which you
have stored up for those who fear you, which you
bestow in the sight of men on those who take
refuge in you. In the shelter of your presence you
hide them from the intrigues of men; in your
dwelling you keep them safe from accusing tongues.

Psalm 31:19–20

$\mathcal{L}$ORD, you establish peace for us; all that we have accomplished you have done for us.

Isaiah 26:12

❧

$\mathcal{L}$et all who take refuge in you be glad; let them ever sing for joy. Spread your protection over them, that those who love your name may rejoice in you. For surely, O LORD, you bless the righteous; you surround them with your favor as with a shield.

Psalm 5:11–12

*R*estore us, O God; make your face shine
upon us, that we may be saved.

Psalm 80:3

❧

*R*estore us again, O God our Savior, and put
away your displeasure toward us. Will you be
angry with us forever? Will you prolong your anger
through all generations? Will you not revive us
again, that your people may rejoice in you? Show
us your unfailing love, O LORD, and grant us your
salvation. I will listen to what God the LORD will
say; he promises peace to his people. Surely his
salvation is near those who fear him, that his
glory may dwell in our land.

Psalm 85: 4–9

Prayers of Praise, Adoration, and Joy

O LORD, God of Israel, there is no God like you in heaven above or on earth below—you who keep your covenant of love with your servants who continue wholeheartedly in your way.

1 Kings 8:23

I will always have hope; I will praise you more and more. My mouth will tell of your righteousness, of your salvation all day long, though I know not its measure. I will come and proclaim your mighty acts, O Sovereign LORD; I will proclaim your righteousness, yours alone.

Psalm 71:14–16

❧

*Y*ou are my God, and I will give you thanks; you are my God, and I will exalt you. Give thanks to the LORD, for he is good; his love endures forever.

Psalm 118:28–29

*H*ow great you are, O Sovereign LORD! There is no one like you, and there is no God but you.

2 Samuel 7:22

❧

O LORD, God of Israel, enthroned between the cherubim, you alone are God over all the kingdoms of the earth. You have made heaven and earth.

2 Kings 19:15

❧

*B*ecause your love is better than life, O LORD, my lips will glorify you. I will praise you as long as I live, and in your name I will lift up my hands.

Psalm 63:3–4

$\mathscr{B}$lessed be your glorious name, and may it be exalted above all blessing and praise. You alone are the LORD. You made the heavens, even the highest heavens, and all their starry host, the earth and all that is on it, the seas and all that is in them. You give life to everything, and the multitudes of heaven worship you.

Nehemiah 9:5–6

❧

$\mathscr{I}$ will praise you forever for what you have done; O Lord, in your name I will hope, for your name is good. I will praise you in the presence of your saints.

Psalm 52:9

Great and marvelous are your deeds, LORD God Almighty. Just and true are your ways, King of the ages. Who will not fear you, O LORD, and bring glory to your name? For you alone are holy. All nations will come and worship before you, for your righteous acts have been revealed.

Revelation 15:3–4

❧

I will praise you, O LORD, with all my heart; I will tell of all your wonders. I will be glad and rejoice in you; I will sing praise to your name, O Most High.

Psalm 9:1–2

$\mathcal{I}$will praise you, O LORD, among the nations; I will sing of you among the peoples. For great is your love, reaching to the heavens; your faithfulness reaches to the skies. Be exalted, O God, above the heavens; let your glory be over all the earth.

Psalm 57:9–11

❧

$\mathcal{I}$will praise you with the harp for your faithfulness, O my God; I will sing praise to you with the lyre, O Holy One of Israel. My lips will shout for joy when I sing praise to you—I, whom you have redeemed.

Psalm 71:22–23

*T*he heavens praise your wonders, O LORD,
your faithfulness too, in the assembly of the holy
ones. For who in the skies above can compare
with the LORD? Who is like the LORD among the
heavenly beings? In the council of the holy ones
God is greatly feared; he is more awesome than
all who surround him. O LORD God Almighty,
who is like you? You are mighty, O LORD, and
your faithfulness surrounds you.

Psalm 89:5–8

I will praise you, O LORD, with all my heart; before the "gods" I will sing your praise. I will bow down toward your holy temple and will praise your name for your love and your faithfulness, for you have exalted above all things your name and your word.

Psalm 138:1–2

❧

I will exalt you, my God the King; I will praise your name for ever and ever. Every day I will praise you and extol your name for ever and ever. Great is the LORD and most worthy of praise; his greatness no one can fathom.

Psalm 145:1–3

*Y*ou are worthy, our Lord and God, to receive glory and honor and power, for you created all things, and by your will they were created and have their being.

Revelation 4:11

❧

O Lord, you are my God; I will exalt you and praise your name, for in perfect faithfulness you have done marvelous things, things planned long ago.

Isaiah 25:1

*P*raise be to you, O L ORD, God of our father Israel, from everlasting to everlasting. Yours, O L ORD, is the greatness and the power and the glory and the majesty and the splendor, for everything in heaven and earth is yours. Yours, O L ORD, is the kingdom; you are exalted as head over all. Wealth and honor come from you; you are the ruler of all things. In your hands are strength and power to exalt and give strength to all. Now, our God, we give you thanks, and praise your glorious name.

1 Chronicles 29:10–13

Prayers of Recommitment

I will remember the deeds of the LORD; yes, I will remember your miracles of long ago. I will meditate on all your works and consider all your mighty deeds. Your ways, O God, are holy.

Psalm 77:11–13

As the deer pants for streams of water, so my soul pants for you, O God. My soul thirsts for God, for the living God. These things I remember as I pour out my soul: how I used to go with the multitude, leading the procession to the house of God, with shouts of joy and thanksgiving among the festive throng. Why are you downcast, O my soul? Why so disturbed within me? Put your hope in God, for I will yet praise him, my Savior and my God. By day the Lord directs his love, at night his song is with me—a prayer to the God of my life.

Psalm 42:1–2, 4–5, 8

*I*n my distress I called to the LORD, and he answered me. From the depths of the grave I called for help, and you listened to my cry. You brought my life up from the pit, O LORD my God. When my life was ebbing away, I remembered you, LORD, and my prayer rose to you, to your holy temple. Those who cling to worthless idols forfeit the grace that could be theirs. But I, with a song of thanksgiving, will sacrifice to you. What I have vowed I will make good. Salvation comes from the LORD.

Jonah 2:2, 6–9

❧

*H*ave mercy on me, O God, according to your unfailing love; according to your great compassion blot out my transgressions. Wash away all my iniquity and cleanse me from my sin. For I know my transgressions, and my sin is always before me. Against you, you only, have I sinned and done what is evil in your sight, so that you are proved right when you speak and justified when you judge. Cleanse me with hyssop, and I will be clean; wash me, and I will be whiter than snow. Create in me a pure heart, O God, and renew a steadfast spirit within me. Restore to me the joy of your salvation and grant me a willing spirit, to sustain me. O LORD, open my lips, and my mouth will declare your praise.

Psalm 51:1–4, 7, 10, 12, 15

O LORD, I remember the days of long ago; I meditate on all your works and consider what your hands have done. I spread out my hands to you; my soul thirsts for you like a parched land.

Psalm 143:5–6

PRAYERS OF STRENGTH

I love you, O LORD, my strength.
Psalm 18:1

O my Strength, I watch for you; you, O God, are
my fortress, my loving God. You will go before me.
Psalm 59:9–10

*Y*ou are awesome, O God, in your sanctuary;
the God of Israel gives power and strength
to his people. Praise be to God!

Psalm 68:35

❧

*I*n your unfailing love, O LORD, you will lead
the people you have redeemed. In your strength
you will guide them to your holy dwelling.

Exodus 15:13

❧

*B*e exalted, O LORD, in your strength;
we will sing and praise your might.

Psalm 21:13

O LORD, be not far off; O my Strength, come quickly to help me. Deliver my life from the sword.

Psalm 22:19–20

❧

*D*eliver me, O my God, from the hand of the wicked, from the grasp of evil and cruel men. For you have been my hope, O Sovereign LORD, my confidence since my youth.

Psalm 71:4–5

❧

O LORD, be gracious to us; we long for you. Be our strength every morning, our salvation in time of distress.

Isaiah 33:2

O LORD, my strength and my fortress, my refuge in time of distress, to you the nations will come.

Jeremiah 16:19

❧

*B*ecause you are my help, I sing in the shadow of your wings. My soul clings to you O LORD; your right hand upholds me.

Psalm 63:7–8

❧

O LORD, whom have I in heaven but you? And earth has nothing I desire besides you. My flesh and my heart may fail, but God is the strength of my heart and my portion forever.

Psalm 73:25–26

PRAYERS OF SUPPLICATION

O God, you are my God, earnestly I seek you; my soul thirsts for you, my body longs for you, in a dry and weary land where there is no water.

Psalm 63:1

*T*urn your ear to me, O God, come quickly
to my rescue; be my rock of refuge,
a strong fortress to save me.

Psalm 31:2

❧

*M*ay all who seek you rejoice and be glad in
you; may those who love your salvation always
say, "Let God be exalted!" Yet I am poor and
needy; come quickly to me, O God. You are my
help and my deliverer; O LORD, do not delay.

Psalm 70:4–5

*I*n you, O LORD, I have taken refuge; let me never be put to shame. Rescue me and deliver me in your righteousness; turn your ear to me and save me. Be my rock of refuge, to which I can always go; give the command to save me, for you are my rock and my fortress. Deliver me, O my God, from the hand of the wicked, from the grasp of evil and cruel men. For you have been my hope, O Sovereign LORD, my confidence since my youth. Do not cast me away when I am old; do not forsake me when my strength is gone. Be not far from me, O God; come quickly, O my God, to help me.

Psalm 71:1–5, 9, 12

*H*ear, O LORD, and answer me, for I am poor and needy. Guard my life, for I am devoted to you. You are my God; save your servant who trusts in you. Have mercy on me, O LORD, for I call to you all day long. Bring joy to your servant, for to you, O LORD, I lift up my soul. You are forgiving and good, O LORD, abounding in love to all who call to you. Hear my prayer, O LORD; listen to my cry for mercy. In the day of my trouble I will call to you, for you will answer me. Teach me your way, O LORD, and I will walk in your truth; give me an undivided heart, that I may fear your name.

Psalm 86:1–7, 11

*S*how me your ways, O L<small>ORD</small>, teach me
your paths; guide me in your truth and teach me,
for you are God my Savior, and my hope
is in you all day long.

Psalm 25:4–5

❧

O God, open my eyes that I may see
wonderful things in your law.

Psalm 119:18

*S*earch me, O God, and know my heart;
test me and know my anxious thoughts. See if
there is any offensive way in me, and lead
me in the way everlasting.

Psalm 139:23–24

❧

*T*each me, O LORD, to follow your decrees;
then I will keep them to the end. Give me
understanding, and I will keep your law and
obey it with all my heart. Direct me in the path
of your commands, for there I find delight.

Psalm 119:33–35

PRAYERS OF THANKSGIVING

*W*e give thanks to you, LORD God Almighty, the One who is and who was, because you have taken your great power and have begun to reign.

Revelation 11:17

*T*hanks be to God! He gives us the victory through our Lord Jesus Christ.

1 Corinthians 15:57

*W*e give thanks to you, O God, we give
thanks, for your Name is near; men tell
of your wonderful deeds.

Psalm 75:1

❧

*Y*ou turned my wailing into dancing; you
removed my sackcloth and clothed me with joy,
that my heart may sing to you and not be silent.
O LORD my God, I will give you thanks forever.

Psalm 30:11–12

❧

*Y*ou make me glad by your deeds, O LORD; I sing
for joy at the works of your hands. How great are
your works, O LORD, how profound your thoughts!

Psalm 92:4–5

I thank and praise you, O God of my fathers.
Daniel 2:23

≈

I will praise you, O LORD, with all my heart; I will tell of all your wonders. I will be glad and rejoice in you; I will sing praise to your name, O Most High.
Psalm 9:1–2

≈

O LORD, my lips will shout for joy when I sing praise to you—I, whom you have redeemed.
My tongue will tell of your righteous acts all day long, for those who wanted to harm me have been put to shame and confusion.
Psalm 71:23–24

O God, we give you thanks, and praise
your glorious name.
1 Chronicles 29:13

❧

I will sing of the LORD's great love forever; with
my mouth I will make your faithfulness known
through all generations. I will declare that your
love stands firm forever, that you established
your faithfulness in heaven itself.
Psalm 89:1–2

❧

Y ou are my God, and I will give you thanks; you
are my God, and I will exalt you. Give thanks to the
LORD, for he is good; his love endures forever.
Psalm 118:28–29

Prayers
of Trust

I trust in your unfailing love, O Lord; my
heart rejoices in your salvation.

Psalm 13:5

*M*ay your unfailing love rest upon us,
O Lord, even as we put our hope in you.

Psalm 33:22

*W*hen I am afraid, I will trust in you.
In God, whose word I praise, in God I trust;
I will not be afraid.

Psalm 56:3–4

❧

*L*et the morning bring me word of your
unfailing love, O LORD, for I have put my trust
in you. Show me the way I should go, for
to you I lift up my soul.

Psalm 143:8

*T*he LORD is my shepherd, I shall not be in want.
He makes me lie down in green pastures, he leads
me beside quiet waters, he restores my soul. He
guides me in paths of righteousness for his name's
sake. Even though I walk through the valley of
the shadow of death, I will fear no evil, for you
are with me; your rod and your staff, they
comfort me. You prepare a table before me in the
presence of my enemies. You anoint my head
with oil; my cup overflows. Surely goodness and
love will follow me all the days of my life, and I
will dwell in the house of the LORD forever.

Psalm 23

I trust in your unfailing love; my heart rejoices in your salvation. I will sing to the LORD, for he has been good to me.

Psalm 13:5–6

❧

T hose who know your name will trust in you, for you, LORD, have never forsaken those who seek you.

Psalm 9:10

*I*n you our fathers put their trust, O God;
they trusted and you delivered them. They cried
to you and were saved; in you they trusted and
were not disappointed.

Psalm 22:4–5

❧

*T*o you, O LORD, I lift up my soul;
in you I trust, O my God.

Psalm 25:1–2

❧

*Y*ou are my refuge and my shield, O LORD;
I have put my hope in your word.

Psalm 119:114

*H*ear my voice when I call, O LORD; be merciful to me and answer me. My heart says of you, "Seek his face!" Your face, LORD, I will seek. Do not hide your face from me, do not turn your servant away in anger; you have been my helper. Do not reject me or forsake me, O God my Savior. Though my father and mother forsake me, the LORD will receive me. Teach me your way, O LORD; lead me in a straight path because of my oppressors. I am still confident of this: I will see the goodness of the LORD in the land of the living.

Psalm 27:7–11, 13

PRAYERS WHEN FACING DIFFICULTY

*I*n the day of my trouble I will call to you,
O God, for you will answer me.

Psalm 86:7

$\mathcal{L}$et all who take refuge in you be glad; let them ever sing for joy. Spread your protection over them, that those who love your name may rejoice in you. For surely, O LORD, you bless the righteous; you surround them with your favor as with a shield.

Psalm 5:11–12

✿

$\mathcal{O}$ut of the goodness of your love, O LORD, deliver me. For I am poor and needy, and my heart is wounded within me.

Psalm 109:21–22

*A*nswer me when I call to you, O my righteous God. Give me relief from my distress; be merciful to me and hear my prayer.

Psalm 4:1

❧

I will lie down and sleep in peace, for you alone, O LORD, make me dwell in safety.

Psalm 4:8

*D*o not withhold your mercy from me, O LORD;
may your love and your truth always protect me.

Psalm 40:11

❧

*B*e pleased, O LORD, to save me; O LORD, come
quickly to help me. May all who seek to take my
life be put to shame and confusion; may all who
desire my ruin be turned back in disgrace.

Psalm 40:13–14

*H*elp us, O God our Savior, for the glory
of your name; deliver us and forgive our sins
for your name's sake.

Psalm 79:9

❧

O LORD, look upon my suffering and deliver me,
for I have not forgotten your law. Defend my
cause and redeem me; preserve my life according
to your promise. Your compassion is great,
O LORD; preserve my life according to your laws.

Psalm 119:153–154, 156

*I*n you, O LORD, I have taken refuge; let me never be put to shame; deliver me in your righteousness. Turn your ear to me, come quickly to my rescue; be my rock of refuge, a strong fortress to save me. For the sake of your name lead and guide me. Free me from the trap that is set for me, for you are my refuge. Into your hands I commit my spirit; redeem me, O LORD, the God of truth. I will be glad and rejoice in your love, for you saw my affliction and knew the anguish of my soul. Be merciful to me, O LORD, for I am in distress; my eyes grow weak with sorrow, my soul

and my body with grief. But I trust in you,
O LORD; I say, "You are my God." My times are in
your hands. Let your face shine on your servant;
save me in your unfailing love. Let me not be put
to shame, O LORD, for I have cried out to you.
How great is your goodness, which you have
stored up for those who fear you, which you
bestow in the sight of men on those who take
refuge in you. Praise be to the LORD, for he
showed his wonderful love to me. You heard my
cry for mercy when I called to you for help.

Psalm 31:1–5, 7, 9, 14–17, 19, 21–22

❧

O LORD, you will keep us safe and
protect us forever.
Psalm 12:7

❧

Look on me and answer, O LORD my God.
Give light to my eyes, or I will sleep in death.
Psalm 13:3

❧

Listen to my prayer, O God, do not ignore my
plea; hear me and answer me. My thoughts
trouble me and I am distraught.
Psalm 55:1–2

*Y*ou are my hiding place O LORD; you
will protect me from trouble and surround
me with songs of deliverance.

Psalm 32:7

*D*o not be far from me, for trouble is near and
there is no one to help. O LORD, be not far off;
O my Strength, come quickly to help me.

Psalm 22:11, 19

*T*hough I walk in the midst of trouble, you, O LORD, preserve my life; you stretch out your hand against the anger of my foes, with your right hand you save me. The LORD will fulfill his purpose for me; your love, O LORD, endures forever—do not abandon the works of your hands.

Psalm 138:7–8

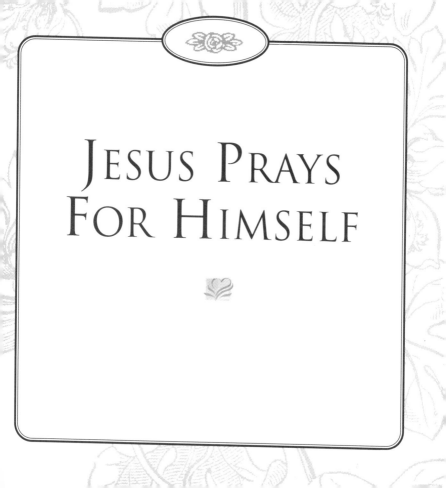

JESUS PRAYS
FOR HIMSELF

$\mathscr{F}$ather, the time has come. Glorify your Son, that your Son may glorify you. For you granted him authority over all people that he might give eternal life to all those you have given him. Now this is eternal life: that they may know you, the only true God, and Jesus Christ, whom you have sent. I have brought you glory on earth by completing the work you gave me to do. And now, Father, glorify me in your presence with the glory I had with you before the world began.

John 17:1–5

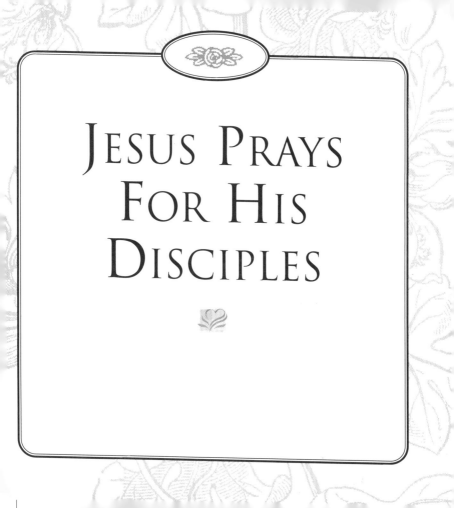

JESUS PRAYS FOR HIS FOR HIS DISCIPLES

❧

I have revealed you to those whom you gave me out of the world. They were yours; you gave them to me and they have obeyed your word. Now they know that everything you have given me comes from you. For I gave them the words you gave me and they accepted them. They knew with certainty that I came from you, and they believed that you sent me. I pray for them. I am not praying for the world, but for those you have given me, for they are yours. All I have is yours, and all you have is mine. And glory has come to me through them. I will remain in the world no longer, but they are still in the world, and I am coming to you. Holy Father, protect them by the power of your name—the name you gave me—so that they may be one as we are one. While I was with them, I protected them and kept them safe by that name you gave me. None has been lost except the one doomed to destruction so that Scripture would be fulfilled.

I am coming to you now, but I say these things while I am still in the world, so that they may have the full measure of my joy within them. I have given them your word and the world has

hated them, for they are not of the world
any more than I am of the world.

My prayer is not that you take them out of the
world but that you protect them from the evil
one. They are not of the world, even as I am not
of it. Sanctify them by the truth; your word is
truth. As you sent me into the world, I have sent
them into the world. For them I sanctify myself,
that they too may be truly sanctified.

John 17:6–19

JESUS PRAYS FOR ALL BELIEVERS

My prayer is not for them alone. I pray also for those who will believe in me through their message, that all of them may be one, Father, just as you are in me and I am in you. May they also be in us so that the world may believe that you have sent me. I have given them the glory that you gave me, that they may be one as we are one: I in them and you in me. May they be brought to complete unity to let the world know that you sent me and have loved them even as you have loved me. Father, I want those you have given me to be with me where I am, and to see my glory, the glory you have given me because you loved me before the creation of the world.

John 17:20–24